Perennial Counterpart

Yongyu Chen

Perennial Counterpart

Nightboat Books
New York

Printed in the United States
ISBN: 978-1-643-62310-8

Cover photograph: Gabby Woo, 2024

Design and composition by Kit Schluter

Typeset in Jacquarda Bastarda 9
and Adobe Caslon Pro

Cataloging-in-publication data is available
from the Library of Congress

Nightboat Books
New York
www.nightboat.org

If the world no longer went on as it does now between man and woman, between truth and lie, like truth now and lie now

If all that went to the devil

If you set out afresh the sum to which you attach value and of which you take account

If you were an airman and, without quibbling, flew your arc, if you only gave news, reports, no more the story of all that together, of yourself and another and a third

Then, if you were whole and no longer wounded, injured, addicted to purity and vengeance . . .

Then, when you no longer think that things must improve "in the framework of the given", that the rich must no longer be rich and the poor no longer be poor, the innocent ought no longer to be condemned and the guilty executed . . .

When at last comes at last

Then

Then jump up once again and tear down the old disgraceful order. Then be different, so that the world shall change, so that it shall change direction, at last! Then embark upon it!

—Ingeborg Bachmann, from "The Thirtieth Year"
translated by Michael Bullock

Contents

Perennial Counterpart

× × ×

Unintelligible to the end. To the end,
unintelligible.

You will not always write. Or, you will always write.

But when I'm dead I will write? Then?

You will not always write.

At some point
some point

at some point the poems will get
better. Then

it will be your expectations, not the poems
that are lacking. Then

you will not write.

You feel

there are other moments. Still there are
other moments, you feel. As if

you could stretch out into the mess of heat
around you, access it.

The first of the series, another series.

Rain removes its head. Who is here?

Frost squeezes out of the sleeve. New moments.

Pull apart the shell—you in general.

If replaced the poem.

You will always write.

05.22.23

Rapidly becoming sick, blanching in the hour before the heat—I am cold in the wind, warmly expanding in the shadow.

It is a pleasure to walk behind you—into a room where I will spend the summer. Be undemanding, diffident even, knowing I can always stand in the space behind the door.

My body will fuse to the cool counter, seeking the oil & pans.

Flat space arches your blood.

My eye. Through its wavering aperture, your head. White foam.

I see the white foam of your sleep cross the shallow grid of morning.

My head, close to the window's vertical slats. Or on the floor by the shoes, looking out from where the room begins.

Bitter & acrid—cooked, the tall grasses will pin down our vanity for ten more years.

Enough time.

You blended the stone with the water. When it cooled, the particulates settled at the bottom of the glass. It was drinkable again. Stone leaving water, they will not mix.

You don't have to think about the brain. It thinks. It settles.

Superject, Undercommons

It's May. I

become accidental,

When
can I visit, you

can say no. Wearing dresses, drinking
clear summer wine, loosening
the petrification
from the spark. In the city

I leave
the movie theater alone. Desire
is the layer
of cells right in front
of my face, a
brain, it's May. I read

the poem we wrote. Leaves

of watermelon growing from the poem we wrote. We wrote *You will be part of your friend's face. You will be part of your friend's face. You will be part of your friend's face.*

//

When I

don't know the word for
what I'm

doing with

you what
am I doing with you?
When

I don't know
where the mistake is

I know
I can just make one. Nave,

clerestory. Why. By

next year I would like to
not
be here. Nor I. Nor be. We

eat in the rain. Experiment

in living. Experiment in living. Experiment in living.

Partager—in one word, both *divide* and *share*.

Deleuze said—write *and* instead of *is*. The question is Relation not Being. Relation not Being.

Antineocolonial modes. Abolition of a society
where this society was possible.

Old friends this is my new friend. It will never make sense. Queerness, something is sharing

us. Yes I got you a gift, no you don't have to open it.

There was a hole in a garden on Prentiss, near Beacon. It rained recently, I wondered if the rain washed it away, should I go check.

For you.

I build a library for a child.

Pendulum

It does not seem like anything separates us, or will. Always will I

love your work as well. In the winding of space & time don't
you think summer opens tunnels. Won't there be
tunnels against the winding,

dear.

    Tunnels, cutting through the sweet dried loaf pressed
    with flowers, through liquid ivy, through Libra, most
    trustworthy of constellations. The entire cliffside overgrown
    with purple ramps, tunneled. When you are cloaked in an aura
    of pain, I will have the right to step behind you. Through one
    of many tunnels. To not be mesmerized by your expression's
    constant altering. And help you upright. The inside

    of the tunnel—I remember it buzzing ripe with condensation.

The winding, the tunnels, the nets (by the shore, the house
covered in nets, in the musk of nets)—

it does not matter which I love more, all traces of the same
endless process.

I write: *ball of flesh with, at its center, a cool, blue liquid.*

I write: *in the tenebrous valley my back looks like a larger heart
held up by white sticks.*

I never imagined we wouldn't be friends. Grey wool
of the binding cloth patrolled by drops of blood.

On the windy day I tie the scarf around my neck tight,
tighter. Its ends brush, through my shirt, my nipples.

In the summer, suddenly—I see traces of a world of ice. Beams,
structures, an entire shadow knowledge not inside summer but

involved with its motion, at the still point of summer.

A great frost.

Pasolini and Callas

When their faces were next to each other they looked older than they were, more sensitive.

When the right person is next to me I can see the abyss.

The creation of a secret. *Secretum*—meaning

also separation. I

can't see the abyss, I can't. I can't see the abyss. Green flowers grow from bread.

Something very wrong. Everything could be so easy. Unlike this.

The middle of the day is almost night.

I know where I am by the smell

of flowers. When the wind blows I think I'm somewhere else, I recalibrate. Being not always

where I think I am, where I am

thickening. Aster, disaster. Aster,

disaster. Bliss.

Your gaze on this page.

Line after line. Each their own length. Furrows. Ease.

How easy everything could be. The ease of speaking with the right person, suddenly, even if we've never spoken before. Don't need to think, no need for will. At each point of the rocky shore, desert and sea melding into a singularly gentle, glowering blankness. A secret. *(A*, meaning not one but

other than one. *A*.) Anyone at all. Pasolini and Callas on the beach.

What does the next word look like to each word. Trees fruiting through the tomb's open kitchen window, pushing in. The fruit invisible. The hard shell.

05.17.22, letter to Yun Qin

Theory of Mesh

There has to be a part of nonpossession that's still relation.
There has to be a purity without closedness. Purity

almost without consciousness, loneliness, pure energy, a pure
person, S—*I hope to sustain always an energy that's very pure.*

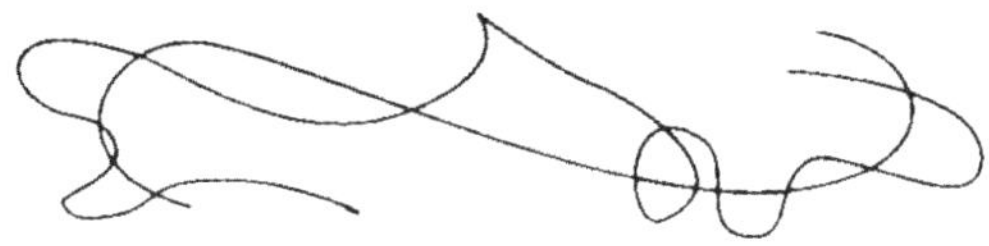

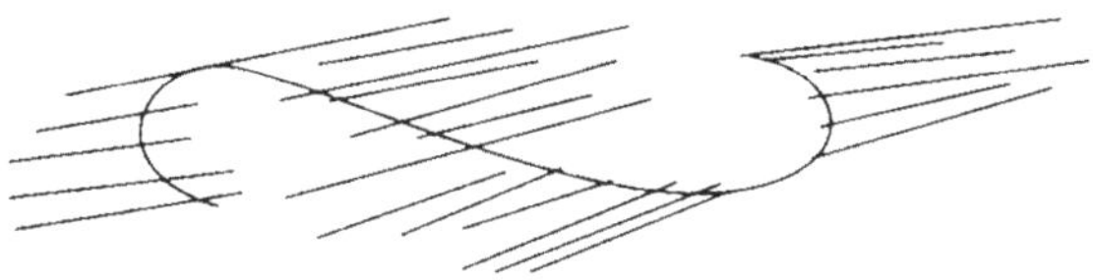

I had spent a year trying to write only in long lines.

I thought, I will write a Lucie Brock-Broido line but even
longer. I will write a poem obsessed

with nights in fields. Duration. Thought. Then

I read a book by Mei-mei Berssenbrugge. I realized
what I was writing was a Mei-mei Berssenbrugge line. When

things like this happen I
know why I'm writing. Theory

of mesh. I came back

to New York. There was a collection of Rachel
Kushner's essays in every bookstore. In each one I reread

her essay on Duras. *Things happened to Duras*, Kushner writes,
that she never experienced. The story of Duras and the older

Chinese lover, for instance, *a legend which, having ripened*
during her whole life, finally

became true in *The Lover*. Her best book. Which means she had to

write it until it was. *Is*. As,
I think, does Kushner. In her novels, with

her life, in her own way. As do I. It's why I love her essay. In

Brooklyn I was visiting H's place & their roommate C told us

about Leonora Carrington. In C's print
of *And Then We Saw the Daughter of the Minotaur*, who,

C asks, is the Minotaur's daughter. I think it's the dancer
the dogs see, I love the dogs. C says, the Minotaur's daughter could be

everything we see after we look away. Maybe. That
much. Looking away is everything. Maybe. At the center

of looking away, being gone

is everything. Maybe. Leonora H. Kushner. Mei-mei

C. Duras. *It was true: I didn't come here to not fall in love*. Writes Kushner of New York. In the mesh

who is she talking to. In a dream

my family photos were taped onto photos
of the distant star and then, as the dream

reached its point of inflection, I realized the star could see us
through our backsides, and,

somehow, S was part of it, S was part of the dream, then part
of the star, part of the seeing,

by being the one outside it, the one

element of waking. In her note at the end
of *Empathy* Berssenbrugge writes—*I was living alone*

in northern New Mexico. Writes—*I met Georgia*
O'Keeffe, Agnes Martin. Writes—*I wanted to feminize scientific language*

and philosophic language.
Writes—*The slow arc of the sun*

across "empty" land became long, poetic lines. Friendship

as a way of life.

Being-together-alone.

And then we saw the daughter of the Minotaur.

The key to all the work up to this point.

for Yun Qin

The Year of Getting Closer to Steam

Smooth leg, deep dream. When the house is empty you come to the dining room & see

the changes.

What you feel, you feel,

is the sheath.

One year you did not visit your parents, which made it three years you did not try.

On your birthday they came. They took you to the rocky beach with dolphins in the water. And you asked father what those bushes were. Heavy, pink flowers,

wild roses, eglantine.

With my friend I talk, we talk, we keep talking.

It is generational in the dusk, like we will pass the conversation to two others, like we even

will pick who. Like we will implant in them the feelings.

They will be this conversation's *finishers*. You can't leave.

But how can I leave? How, how can I leave?

The rules are empty, they are the giant, empty space.

The bath is filled with cool water, speaking back & forth with your body.

Remove your ideas. In the blinks you remake your winter organs into fish, you make

each vein, you make sure you don't die, even in the version. And even though

you forget the gills you do not correct yourself.

Mathematical proof. Shiny stones.

Cook the thorn.

05.24.23

When you look down your face recedes. It is a pleasure to not follow you
then into the core of your body. A pleasure to stand aside,

by your recession. We sit with your friend, in early summer, at the blue
café, his face pale & transparent like a medusa. You lean

in. And recede in the eager waves of his speech. I recede, parallel to you. I
do not learn the essential things. I do not

move my hands in circles on the wet surface of the essential. I watch the
mark on his face, stable & changing. Climbing

like a cliff. I will never know. I am not a secret either. Earlier, he says,
when you painted in Chicago, his studio next to yours, he saw you

through the doorway, walking to & from the canvas. He saw it as an
intensity. When he took it out of himself it was

an intensity. It surprised him.

for Gabby

Consequential Maneuver

An action, imperceptible in the moment.
Diffuse, gentle. Later, a giant form

overhanging all else. Silent

in the background's

dampness, weaving-in between the lake

& rain, noncommittal, keeping track
of their differences.

Rain strikes the lake. It rises

in ridges of level, each ridge in four

faces. Could, can. Now can't. Again,

can. Lake
freezes from surface
down. Action
complicates.
Ice,
horizontally & vertically,
makes
different marks in me, the second darker
in magnitude, closer
to knowledge. Something
maneuvers
in between.
Not action. Maneuvers
between the actions.

× × ×

I hold onto old connections. Don't you?

This word makes no sense in the evening.

It is said—knowledge is discontinuous droplets. Clouds of ice & rain form a carapace around each droplet. In the cloudcover, enough space for rivulets to branch.

What if—when lightning strikes

against each facet of cloud's defense, it burns up

immediately against the spiritless neck of cloud. Clear, scentless smoke.

Air, filling with humidity, is like snow melt.

I do not think you will be an artist. No.

There is a force in you.

It breaks through.

In you it takes a further step.

Vézelay

after, as Georges Bataille

The wall of summer pitted with walnut shells. Clawed flanks of vine. No windows in the kitchen. A pure sound as storm fell—comfort, the evulsion of, bright forms in the dark.

I had developed a nocturnal vision.

I wished—I had the strength to write, to you, in the form of a list, the people I hated because of my love for you. Very short list. Unknown,

white flutters. Long ago, O told me, they fell asleep, alone in a summer bed filled with their partner's books . . . I see the lightning

cut into the pages between the books, I see what the memory refuses, obsession, anonymity. Most of us.

In the bedroom I close the blinds.

Can you explain this.

Unhappiness is a core like a crystal, a heavy polar axis. It does not make me happier. When I left Paris for the country I thought I had failed, in my life, to make my fear understood.

Friendship. *Are there incompatibilities.*

Even the grass on the stone today begging for newer, loftier morals.

I don't mean rules for action. I don't mean that.

Window divided in two by light, wall divided into feelings. The clouds are so dark. The thunderstorm is an illumination but only for faces. So I see only the faces very clear between the salted blades of grass.

I don't sleep. When dawn comes it feels like rest in its own way. My body knows it should be rested.

I love the nightmare the most. In the nightmare I love the nightmare the most. In the nightmare I only love the nightmare the most.

Light pouring down the wall. I love the light pouring down the wall. In the light pouring down the wall I love only the light pouring down the wall the most. Light pouring & pooling in the corners of morning but in the light I love only the light the most. In the light pouring down the wall I only love you the most. I only love you. Waking. Then, in the kitchen, bringing the grapes to a boil.

for Olivia

Late May, Late June

White wisteria drapes over the mussels. I am unclaimed, sit next to me by the riverbed's pulp,

my counterpart.

Though indistinguishable now we may soon be nothing alike. Your muscles are wrapped by my observant hair, incompatible in texture. If our eyes touch it is a juncture guarded from all other vision

by their conjoined sheen.

In a past summer—someone I knew put violets & ice in a clay pitcher & washed my hair outside. The wind so strong it blew our laptops off the counter. In the Midwest, the storm golden. Now I know no one.

Plenum

Experiences always happened. It's not time to remember yet. Keep going.

I thought, I am no longer having experiences.

But I am walking in the night through Cambridge & no one is on the street. There is no sound. I hear myself speaking.

& I walk past places where things happened. Things happen.

Low lights, at ankle level, cast my shadow onto the undersides of the leaves. Great disparate tissue of all the leaves.

I trust, I am still having experiences.

At this table I sat with R, he introduced me to N, his partner, whom I had heard about all summer. All this happened. For them, through the great disparate tissue of letters. Of postponement. Of arriving at the same place different times.

On the ground by this table, years before, with C I drank wine & listened to music. C listened to me. He understood me.

Always, the steeple lit at night.

Always, the curtain of the gallery pressed loose to the windows, so a band of the room shows through. It's not hidden. It's night. There's nothing to hide.

I jumped the terrace guardrail & sat on its edge with A, with her weed pen, with W. At different times, not together. On the 3rd floor.

That was before night congealed around a smell of horror.

Things fall through the trees.

I will sit next to you & show you my fingers. Ask you, will it not be true, when I'm dead, this band of bone where the ring sits will be glittering among all the rest? All that pressure does something.

Pressure, heat, sound.

I started writing to you tonight, lying down in bed, next to G as she ate the strawberries I washed. Their smell came down to me. I hid under the covers. She had showered. The dampness came in. I spoke to you. You were there.

Bachmann & Jaeggy sit next to each other in an Italian house & she says, isn't life horrible? & she smiles, the other one. & time passes quickly. Time sweeps past in one uniform band. Why not call it a wing?

I will sit next to you & say, pretend they're not there. Look, people around us. Pretend they're not there. Pretend H is not there from your letter. Pretend the Argentine writer is not there, even if his book is, even if you aren't reading it or are, you shouldn't be. There's nothing there. It won't change the world.

I will even say,

pretend the river isn't there. Pretend the city isn't there, the fish, the sudden coldness, the tallness of space in the dark, now even time sweeping past, not there, the wing. Here are my fingers, ten of them, one with its tight, sparkling band beneath. I am not wearing clothes. This is a bench. Nothing is here. Not even the manic swirl of the water.

Language can't punish you.

You can't be defeated by language.

I feel the dampness rising & falling in an empty field. Feel my presence twist the field & twist against it to keep its grid

Euclidean. Feel your presence emit waves into the field.

Those waves are crisp as marble.

Let's strip away parts of your letter, more & more parts.

Our letters were beautiful, intimate. They felt like love letters. You don't need to say it. Pretend that's not there.

& friendship is hard I know. & I too barely speak to people I write to, in person, because writing does something to them . . . pretend it's not there. & even if writing did nothing I would barely speak. Like a chemical in a sterile, glass cup, I will not react.

If there is a beautiful fairytale,

it is one in which, when it ends, the princess

clears away the sentences & builds a stage. She puts us on it. & will design her own conversation. & will make us speak parts of her she ought to clarify. Then when we speak smoke will rise out of our eyes. As we clarify her questions we'll clarify parts of us.

Simple how in German, *Samen* is seed & semen. & *fortpflanzen* to procreate or propagate.

My roommate grew alfalfa sprouts on our balcony & yesterday we ate them. The flies gathered around the bowl & dove in, dove into the shreds of the seeds at the ends.

& there is a word,

vollkommen.

I learn to use it.

Though the curtains

are inside the gallery's glass wall, they move. Outside wind blows through the leaves & they move. They move & slide around the edge of speech. & would not avow anyways.

They are just green & dark & it is not cold.

Ithaca was cold.

Life is horrible isn't it. Isn't life horrible?

Even reading Cavafy gives no pleasure.

& I am happiest when alone & leaning towards others.

So what are you writing now.

That was yesterday.

Tonight I walk to the same table & write.

Telling myself, if it works, I'll do it again. I'll do it until it doesn't work.

Then, find a new pattern.

Today I took the subway to Alewife & walked through the wetland park. & saw clumps of my cabbages in the shallow pond.

So many clumps of stalks.

In the pond, waste.

My teacher hated the phrase *lived experience* because it reminded her it's possible to not live experience.

I'm always waiting. When have I not thought,

I am waiting. I thought,

this summer, this will be the summer I finally can go through with hormones, but it will be fall.

For external reasons, fall.

But it should be summer.

I had imagined summer around me. & touching my mind with my hand. Walking up & down the steps as my features dissolve & loathing the displays of handbags, & spongelike garlands, garlands of leaves.

From a dream, I wake up & call you

Hadrian.

Cavafy & his Alexandrians—I could be more Greek than any of them. If I wanted to, I too could claim the title,

Hellenized.

The poem becomes information & it dies.

But I wanted to tell you.

& am distracted today.

Wanting black silk shorts with drawstrings.

& on the walk home I'll take the longer path, stopping by CVS for G.

She doesn't care how you spell her name. In your head what is she?

Light, gravity, stones, clouds, leaves. Among these very few elements, I drop a name into the Euboean water.

Dark leaves, dark clouds above them, dark sky above. Stringent, vituperative, vengeful?

& again the steeple, bright, crossed over by a butterfly.

& I only notice, now after writing this, that tonight, unlike last night, there is no wind. No leaves move.

This morning I fantasized about reading. Book laid on my legs. Legs raised onto the seat of a car that drives me to a beach or field, any flat space, without gaps or flanks. & in front of the leg-glow each page, as it turns, ignites an object in the real world. & now

I will experience calmness.

Gefasst war die Spannung im Gesicht. Gefasst waren die Beine, gekreuzt unter dem Tisch. Geh weg. Komm näher im drehenden Wind. I am not done with even calmness. With even the wick after its burn. I see into the span of the hare's face as it turns back.

The rabbit jumped onto the balcony with her children & they drank her milk in front of me. I heard the sound of them sucking.

Because I could not see I moved closer.

The mother ran, leaving the babies behind. These reacted, more slowly, but they ran.

I left the terrace. & as I left walked past the mother. She looked at me.

& as I walked home it is the car that sped past as I waved at it, not stopping for me—that is the person I would kill.

06.12.24, letter to Peter

Truant

Even a word gains resonance.

In my vision I died.
In the rain's middle, night turning.

Maxilla, Premaxilla, Sacrum.
Hilda, Frances, Ezra.

Remember, I am writing for you, I am writing your life.

I became the astronomer's daughter.
Backdrawn American icewater. Resonant

in the slipstream.

There *is* a right time to speak. The felt ends of the lips *do*
gather static. What do you want?

A stalactite with its heart-sac. A friend in the cave. A cord to cut.

One by one, small hoofprints to the side of the paved path, unrolling.
I speak for them.

For M,

for instance, there is no word. Words surround it. It is
a question. Sun reveals leaves in London.

And they sit for hours discussing it.

He sees another kind of life. Sees it
in the non-stillness of its attributes. Sees the storm in the feeble geraniums.

Without moving he dives.

Brush, go the petals.

Even a word like *formless*, like *without form* gains resonance.

The minotaur, seated, aslant in his narrow seat—this breaks. Sleep comes.
The calm light reveals the paths of blood under his skin. He has

no heart.

I looked everywhere.

No heart.

for Mo-Jai

Macerations

The brain's oils and the berry's erasing each other. The pieces of brain and the pieces of fruit mixing until the stretch of sand

is white. A voluminous white without sympathy. Summer makes islands maybe, footpaths gridded with breeze. Who does not deserve

a more complete life. How to speak, how to hold onto the shoulders firmly and not slip, not let go of the friend and speak.

M, it turns out, is thirty-three. At our age they lived in Paris selling feminine hygiene products. They had short hair in winter. In nightclubs they saw

Virginie Despentes, with her then-girlfriend, leaving, clothes trailing behind in macerating trails of light. Open door framing dawn air, welcoming the vinegar dryness.

This gap of ten years is unimaginable. The tart M baked tonight is oily, wonderfully sour.

When I am thirty-three I will be crystal, root systems vulcanized. I will be missed. Woven into the brittle surroundings.

At the party I keep leaving. I sit in the stairwell—what is vivid is the distance. Until I pull out this droplet inside me like violence. Until I harden into the building's impersonal structure.

G keeps finding me, keeps sitting with me, until I want to return.

This night is weddinglike, loose and damp. We stand without shells. Without attributes in the webbed variegations of dark, waves rowing out from the interior.

The next day, dressing in black pants, black shirt. Subdued, remorseful even. But when I taste last night's apple on the morning walk I feel

so acutely,

something inside me and all matter would

revolutionize life. Grey sky.

G and I grow in the afternoon like tomato plants. We grow up. We grow into the year's mollusk shell. We clean the mold from the teacups rising into the afternoon grounds of our eyes.

On the first warm day of the year I walk thirty minutes for wine. Wind laying flat on my skin. A full contact of pain.

Friend—I have seen your mother's face. Unchanging. In the afternoon's slow, complicated progression.

Friend—I have seen my mother's face in summer hanging two gutted fish side by side before the shaded kitchen's window. The Tennessee River flooding. The lights went off.

You must stand in the explanation's center, dead-on.

I am not in nor of the light. I am divided by the light. Each division divided in turn in the mothering proliferations of light. In the light which will not, will not ever let me rest. Which tells of me

back to people I know.

A sequence of past selves lined up, each next to a river of identifications. Say—these, these are the fascinations.

We say the same things to each other. I must take care of you in my own way.

for Mar

Squall Path

The low shell holds me down in cramped space. So, we're communicating?

But notice, grey fibers linking on with what we say.

Are there two options?

Patty, I learned everything from you. I can't choose. I imitated your feelings. I liked what you liked. The wall by the candle gently warm, I step into it. My brainstem becomes part of the mold. All else mere backtow

even if massive. Sparrow-winged-angelic

with growth. I can't decide for you. I can transform your memories. I test what is true in your idea.

Thinner fibers—yellow, green, purple—gain on the woolen grey, link on with it—

Your letter reaches me, second week of January, as night rain melts snow field.

I walk in the mixture, I river around. I trawl an experience to attach it to. Wet all over, dry

still in the stomach's crook.

This is my experience. I take off my glasses.

The subject shatters—go further. What shape, how far the lightest pieces travel on the newly washed, polished floor.

The heavy doors close on the light.

The room grows empty, saturated with deep niches. My heart will spend the night in the library.

So we're communicating, squallow mother, across the unsustainable poem-extraction.

01.11.24, for Patty

Nessuno (Not One)

As it happened—it was

harder to read her stories the further I got
in the *Collected Stories*. It was not

gradual, actually. I was

reading her in German, to practice my German, to climb
up to her. My prepositions sparkled. My teacher

smiled at me in the teetering density. Then
her language, it

flew, literally flew out of my grasp—so what was she
learning? Around this time

it was like a dam breaking

& my body, all of a sudden, started to transform.
My breasts grew & the bed held them. I wore

the necklace on the rain day & my scarf wrapped above it &
the neckline of my shirt was below it & my sweater, too large, further below—

four lines, each in its stratum,
broke. And clouds entered the conduit.

I have thought about things that accumulate then transform. And those
that accumulate & never transform. I

prefer the latter, because
it is secret. And

think, difficulty seeps out of the deepest layer to rise through
to the surface, sieved through

by other layers. I don't, don't

know the last line of this poem, & it rises through what I write.
    Bachmann
did you like, as child,

how other children called you
the Owl? & the name did not break, so did not

leave you. Neither does the other name.

The last book is the hardest. Is this why it's the last? Unfissurable,
    gleaming
enameled color.

No heavy touch.
No, not anywhere.

I am not always on my side since I have other commitments & you do not
    need to worry about me.

But I want to *feel* it.

Monarchy of the North

As time relates to time do I have my own relation.

Rain for four days. The dry dream. My phone glittering like hair, my friend texts *I wish we lived closer together*, the shower steaming.

In the old quarters narrow medieval streets. Consent to look away from the world.

The dream had no parts, I believe, no particulars. Only dryness's constant pull.

Your face appeared, emulsive and blurred in its dissidence, in its dissidence to my dreaming, in profile, unpartitioned, a pure upright resistance.

When it ended the face did not leave the dream.

Am I a component of time.

I see the components locking onto each other on the empty plane. Windswept by grass.

I am not a component of time. I dream our friendship's flesh in this, my poem of granite, and eat it. I fantasize about it ending.

Still I would like my own relation to time.

The black Gothic buttresses straddling the Romanesque wings of the nave in this city near the forest in Portugal. Cold as the peel's night lemon.

G and I drive here. We drive from the waves to the books. We leave the cat behind. We think we bring the waves with us. A single memory, a smell like knowing.

Later when sun hits the memory, it becomes matte, neutral. It spreads into the waves. It encases them in armor. It instaurates feeling's defense.

Form burning away lines to get to the matter. Form in sunlight. When there was sunlight.

The rain's power, our matching scarves, wool shining in its attentiveness, we have sex.

We have sex, we talk about the sex we will have, in public, in a friend's room while they sleep. And we can't sleep.

Sick the next morning.

The dark star of elegance. Elegant as we remember the sun.

We said, then, *in the sunscape, skin & temples show, heads show through—our lives are perfect.*

Sunclaws eyesmud.

Maybe they are the same reality. Maybe they are not the same but they are pages in a book next to each other.

Continuity so dark it is scary. So close to the ligature there is no space for light in-between.

Knowledge

I read your letter last night
I slept

& in my dream felt the need to rest, immense the pull towards rest.
I was dying of old age. And if I wanted to live, I could, but I would have
to resist the resting. It was like making

my entire body vibrate with waking. Waking the dream
comprehends. I was lying down. I could lift my head
to look down at my body. Like this I lived. The dream took me

somewhere else through its cerulean channel.

The dying felt good, not unwelcome
to the senses, & was true. A true dying.

It helped me not be afraid.

The resisting felt self-contained.
If I

resist & in the resisting

resist the resisting would it be like listening? Here is the song. It leaves.

Even in Boston is the sea
primordial.

I have been going there with N, my new friend, to read.

I tell N what I like about her poems & it is not what she likes.
And her poems change, & become like my poems. And she tells me

what she likes about my poems, which is not what I like,
so I have to let it change me.

The rocks on the shore, each covered with its snails, *primordial.*

I wrote to my teacher about reading Bolaño's poem by the sea
& his response did not have as much love for me as mine for him

because it was shorter. And,

at the end of the email, he said

he missed, or that we were missing,

his presence, missing his words

on the past fifty years.

And the email ended:

We'll count on you to carry forward poetry's non-power from here.

And I felt

MISUNDERSTOOD.

× × ×

No hope in the image of two people, knowing each other well,
counting on each other.

What about two, knowing each other well, counting
on a stranger, a blank space?

That is not quite it either.

That's not where the problem is.

I lie down, cold in the day in my room, in my jacket, & look at my body.

11.27.24, letter to Peter

Poetics

When I perceive you what does it look like. What does perceiving look
like. If I could perceive you but remove the you,

what would it look like.

What would happen.

Scintillating. Flashes

of light inside my nerves when I perceive you. On the phone with you. Flashes

of heart inside the water. Without heart. Without water. Flashes. Without
light. Without eyes. Without love. What else. What would it look like. Space

contracting into attention. Pointed at you in the fog. Beyond you.
Intensity. Nets of intensity.

The next time I'll see you is 2024.

The night before you left New York we tried to find a book by Bachmann.
Any book by Bachmann. It was her that mattered, her we could share. I
had not

thought about this since it happened.

When you told me I remembered it again. Flashes. When I remember it I
see *dark*, *city*, *winter coats*, pastness runs through its visible arteries. In

all of New York, a book by her, incredible

to circle around a thing, get closer to something

not there. I

had not forgotten it. It was in me. It was dissolved in me. When you told me I felt it crystallize in me. I felt its string of crystals. Moving through the greyness of my body.

On the phone you tell me you hear the birds around me. Suddenly they're deafening. To me. On the phone you are telling me

you are *falling in love*. Earlier in a letter

you quote Lispector. *In the palm of his hands he no longer holds an octagon but a miracle. From this moment onwards he no longer sees anything. He possesses it.*

Flashes. Burning sea. Flashes. Coral trapped in stone. Trying to grow away from

the fossil. The quote was about love. For you the quote

was about love. Flashes. You tell me—in the past you wrote about love trying to perceive it. Now you possess it. Now you are passing from perceiving to possessing. You are dissolving love in you. It has to do

with waiting and doing. Then, not waiting, not doing. Then

long sentences in a long novel. And, I think,

thinking—how thinking burns perceiving, how it burns possessing, burns the membrane between them. This membrane. This membrane

between perceiving and possessing. This is what scares me. In bed. At noon. Dreaming of a boat covered in spiders. After

the journey, in a house that looks like us. I love

to tell you what you told me. I love

to tell you what you told me so you remember it. So you know how it feels to pass to the other side of your telling. So it remains undissolved a little longer. So when it dissolves

in you it dissolves all this time it took. A glass bottle's opening.

Bachmann and New York. Years ago.

Now you are translating her into Chinese. You are living in Beijing where I was born. I

think of all the people who will read her through you. When I think

of perception I think

living with. I think about living together. I think

of another person I love, who I want to live with. If

I perceive you we are living together? If I possess you we are living together? I am no longer sure possession means what I think it means. I am learning something here. Not about you. Or me. Or the person I love. Or you love. But the strange one. Strange, like Malina, strange.

Every March I think about the same things.

I don't know.

Perceiving, possessing, perceiving again. Crystallizing, dissolving, crystallizing again.

The fur that grows on the crystal.

Innocence.

The stars at each point of each star.

I'm sitting alone at home and thread a sheet of paper into the typewriter, without thinking I type: Death will come.

04.04.22, *letter to Yun Qin*

Self-Portrait at 26

The old city of Barcelona, the park on the mount, *yes, I remember.*

My friend who was sick. Then I was sick. And the hot water ran. Too long. The landlord came down, angry, & we denied it. And sat in the bar in the daytime with orange juice, the keys in my pocket large, unwieldy. And I helped him wet napkins for his eyes, which burned from fever & yes,

Calle Tallers, where Bolaño lived.

Some things spread out, deplace.

We go to the beach. We are now at the beach.

What we do there connects to other people, I tell them about it & they don't respond. They are patient, maybe. For years, waiting. Building the thick shell before they shed it in front of me.

The rocks are green at sunset on the shore. When they dry they are grey. No one comes down from the path to the beach, so we observe them, on their contained path above.

Then we are sitting by the fort. Its two wings curl around us. We hear everyone in this field. It is strange the water is silent.

We watched *Stalker*. He fell asleep. I watched, in the film, the man falling asleep, head next to the stream with leaves in it. I fell asleep.

My friend called from England the next day. Yes, she had broken up with that man. When she leaned back, she fell almost out of her window. There was a courtyard—pigeons in front of me, & the children of Barcelona were skating. And it was dawn.

In Ithaca there was a bed large enough for me & another to sleep on, by the waterfall, & not touch. Those white curtains. And the crinkling seam. Sunset, scraping clean the body's tissue. The waterfall walks up to me now, revivified, & looks me in the eye, face in my face, pouring past.

They are an artist now, that person.

I am incorruptible, protected always.

The moon, the moon.

I fall asleep in the feeling & wrinkle it. And slow it down. And make the notch for another feeling to lie above it, awry, locked in place.

Roberto Bolaño earned 2,400 pesetas but when he checked he had only 2,200. Where had the rest gone? Now, the people who know him are dying.

The biography will be lost. I write to the professor I miss.

Dalí kisses Lorca. His mouth is seawater & medicine bubbling. He comes up to me with a photo, rolls it out, asks, *are you hers?*

Yes, she is my mother.

He is Hypnos & René Char & rolls out the long book & points at the words. Artemis? I am hers. Eurydice? Hers. He points at himself.

Yes, I am you, little boy.

I was known by that name.

If I had to buy words to write? I need *byssus*, *arcosolium*, *lunette* . . . D. A. Powell's, the book I am reading. If I can't write I would put the writing in living & write there.

And if I am sick the next time we meet? There is still the cemetery, & music.

A song I think of but won't talk about, because it will disintegrate, I think of it wildly. Its raised edges rise & join into the channel, the direct channel.

Walking parallel to it, I saw the highway fill up into paths of ocean water, with fish-cars.

All of life will go here. It will make it whole into the poem.

Z, to whom I gave the bear of my name, broke up with me & moved to Berlin. R & I broke up in Berlin & I cried in the Starbucks & wrote a poem. A man from Australia spoke to me. Or, I walked up to him & spoke. And what will I do if I return?

Magnetic sun. I will burn the marigolds at the nexus with your hand.

The apartment smelled like cigarettes in the morning but with sweetness, like the stones I sat on did that.

I left my room for a day. I slept for a night, & there was the fruit fly. The plum left on my desk had bruised, & still it was tasteless. Still it was soft & ready, & without taste.

Salvador Dalí, I am touched you have this photo.

for Nicola

Mouse Song

After the dream of a white bed topped with a pool of water,
where in that dream I took photos of the white bed & the water,
look at the crushed flowers afloat in the water . . .
that same night I dreamt I was a child again, I threw a fit, I
rolled on the carpet of the governmental office, in front of both
officials, I beat my water bottle on the ground
I was
last in line at the close of day, they skipped me though
I saw
there was time.

Sing with me, sing with me the mouse song . . .

All Saxony a flood through which the chilled leaves of nettle rose,
heavy with water—*coins!, coins!*—I give you half, you lend me yours,
I buy horses & briny, French hair bows . . . the shopkeepers smile—
who will counterdict us?

Though we danced we watched the better dancers bend out of shape,
these separated, moved towards the corners,
the strands of their hair tore apart, we held them & though
they did not cry, we made pain.

I deserve nothing? I? I?

There is so much intuition left on the exposed outcrops. Won't we scrape it off the beams, the split plinths, until nothing is left?

You are not a streak of grease on a larger tongue, my long, loose children. You are unstuck. You coat the mechanism of the clock tower with a muddy glow. Go. Go. You smooth the passage of blank hooves into heaven.

Flightpath

The tiny crystals growing between the threads of my sweater

are crystals of thought. When I

press my hand against me I feel them.

⌘ ⌘ ⌘

So I wrote—

Thought is the flightpath of the outside
through the waypoints
of my body.

Through the quiescence of my body.

⌘ ⌘ ⌘

A tenu, a tenew—the unit of tenuousness. Faint dusk exists. So summer doesn't. For now. Love, strands of love from my table
in the empty café connecting to
the next.
Empty café.

I thought the first half of my life had ended. Long drive through the Midwest.

On shuffle, playing all the songs I had ever saved, as many as I could, a

fantastic recapitulation.

There are only
two halves.
Of a life. Once
I say half
there are suddenly
only two halves
of a life.

Tigris, Euphrates,
no. No.

Unreachable.

× × ×

Spider eating the starfish raw, starfish growing back
completely
unwhole
then
completely
whole
within
the spider,
down every
single leg
of spider.

I was so certain. When the wave washes over the starfish the thinnest part of the starfish is the dream.

× × ×

In the new bathroom the sky flashes dark then bright. It too in process of becoming personal. I like to rest here.

The possibility of a quieter sexuality. Orange juice, jam on the cover of the novel. At breakfast. At noon.

Friendships were layers held one above the other &, between the layers, cords, which were not friendships.

This Portuguese dress, its rotten fabric, swells lightly, shreds off at the shoulders, finally almost ceramic in consistency.

I sleep well, waking occasionally to shapes flitting past in deep space. Do you have no ambition?

Tombpetals

Nothing stops.—Closeness, closer. I thought,

Eden as withdrawal, the space opened up behind one, space you know matters because it was only just

not there.—Instead

of *tomb*, I was practicing saying, *the possibility of tombs.*—To see

what happens. Matter

floats, each thing that exists dreams itself something that doesn't, then becomes that possibility. That person, that claustrophobia of lens buried in an architrave

of star.—You

look further and further up the wall

for interiority's source. *The dreamed ones*

are those so good at being thought of, you love them.—This is what I meant when I read it.—Already

the next language could be not a language of images

but an image of language, of what it means to have an idea in language, in other people, intimacy.—I said to my friend, just now,

the best place to put a crystal is writing. Nowhere else does it look so sharp, brilliant.—Like, at Herculaneum, the dark red walls of cinnabar

when the ash dreams, dark blonde grapefruit glittering in a bowl,
gathering insideness.—Some

rooms are so inside the insideness steals away.—Once

you emanate a gentleness you will

come in.

× × ×

On the roof I was flipping through a long Spanish novel but it was so dark
I couldn't see the pages, so dark I read the page by shutting it

against another.—I read,

Norton thought: I have to get out of here. And she scanned the room, trying to pinpoint the exact spot where the woman was, but it was impossible to see her. In order for her to be reflected in both mirrors, she said to herself, she must be just between the little entryway and the room. But she couldn't see her.

We lay down on the floorboards with the window and furniture behind
us.—

Look at the moon. Every single smell. You read me

a love poem by a soldier, not a love poem. Which war? *Yes,*

perception will save the world.

The six of swords.

The lizard biting the boy's finger in Caravaggio's painting, cracks in the wall

filled with magma when dawn breaks.—

Does it exist? We agree to try, hard as we can, to walk backwards while walking forwards. This straining.—

While the trees watch. And, on the counter, clean, empty glasses. Mugs the cat drinks from. And everywhere else.—

Bright walls in a dark room. Bright walls in a dark room. Bright walls in a dark room. Dark room. *What's wrong with my eyes. What's wrong*

with my eyes. They are open and they don't see. They are open and they don't see. And

I

<table>
<tr><td>love</td><td>love</td><td>bright</td><td>bright</td><td>dark</td><td>dark</td></tr>
<tr><td>being</td><td>being</td><td>walls</td><td>walls</td><td>room</td><td>room</td></tr>
<tr><td>here</td><td>here</td><td></td><td></td><td></td><td></td></tr>
<tr><td></td><td></td><td>bright</td><td>bright</td><td>dark</td><td>dark</td></tr>
<tr><td>love</td><td>love</td><td>walls</td><td>walls</td><td>room</td><td>room</td></tr>
<tr><td>being</td><td>being</td><td></td><td></td><td></td><td></td></tr>
<tr><td>here</td><td>here</td><td>bright</td><td>bright</td><td>dark</td><td>dark</td></tr>
<tr><td></td><td></td><td>walls</td><td>walls</td><td>room</td><td>room</td></tr>
<tr><td>love</td><td>love</td><td></td><td></td><td></td><td></td></tr>
<tr><td>being</td><td>being</td><td>bright</td><td>bright</td><td>dark</td><td>dark</td></tr>
<tr><td>here</td><td>here</td><td>walls</td><td>walls</td><td>room</td><td>room</td></tr>
</table>

It was an erosion. It was like an erosion I felt good in. Chandelier

turned inside-out and only then lit, then served on a platter

with vermouth, essence of hibiscus, vinegar. The white lace of the curtain. The sound of a voice porous and loving, someone's and not. Saffron in orange juice.—Do

not go away, do not put mercury in it. I

made breakfast for you.

× × ×

The idea of a screen concealing what's in front of it: opposition between onar *(the common dream) and* hupar*: the grand clear dream, the never believed prophetic vision (Pythia).*

10.27.21, for R

Listening

Years of that poem with the horse coin stuck on the tongue to death . . .
years of that poem on the wall

& what distilled was

appetite.

| X | X | X | X |

Here is a problem, four singulars. And

where the decay was most intense on the inside it would melt the snow on the outside of the body: And

year, year, year, year. (Melting, all.)

And poem.

Dark moon rocks took my friend's place. Now, they

    speak, freely.

Now after delays,

    now as child shadow sleep wraps them around

        in Jean Valentine's ocean. And now the gun

        on the ocean floor . . . happens. Happens.

        Happens. And finally

                                the world.

05.11.23

In the deserted studio of summer I find this cabinet of papers.

It writes—a desire for a blanketing heat, a city conspiring, ambiguously, in acts of killing & revival. A Belgian poet, S.P., transformed into a beam

of vermillion.

There are—photographs of friends, exhibition catalogues from the Renaissance Society. 2019, in Chicago where, G says, she was

as well. I had not expected

to feel

myself linked, by something essential. Adjacent to a person for years, quietly—linked, after all, by something lightly

essential. A way of feeling. A way of reading, emerging

out of a way of feeling, entailing

a set of judgements, self-consistent, i.e., a kind of

love. I give up the thought of being linked to my friends

by what is essential. I give up the regret of not knowing to whom I may be linked

by what is essential. I left the place in disarray.

Is there larger disarray. Summer

is giant, loose & empty as cloth wrinkling over the empty glass. (I write—if there is a friendship that is exactly summer, I am with you coruscating in that friendship that is summer.)

Exactly.

Between the active voice, *nomous tithénai*, "to make laws," as the lawmaker makes laws for the people, activity passing from lawmaker into

the people—&

the middle voice, *nomous tithéstai*, "to make laws" while including oneself, to give laws also to oneself, act only

while acting also on oneself, folding one's subject back

into the verb's process—between them, the polis's street lined with little red flowers.

This application of a force within a volume. That twists the form of the volume. Which, twisting, twists as well

what is around it. A new

law—up to now everything indecisive, cautious. Faced

with the snakes in the thundering grove is there—why could there not be—a way to act not starting with the snake?

Around language—what is it—that giant mass, darkly calcifying, now obdurate, but not unalterable.

Later it was the sun showing through the long, cold cracks of train.

Ithaca-Thiais

Die Welt ist fort, ich muß dich tragen.

You measure out a space.

To the side you measure another,

not knowing what is habitable.

Accurately you take its measure.

The grey pit stone of my body cramps beneath fingernails, beneath fabric already sheer as feasible, beneath long black hairs capsizing into the knuckle's crease. Is this habitable?

× × ×

Heat broke. Clumps of wet parsley unchopped on the counter, left—swallowed in expanding, booklike grey. We left, we came back elsewhere. We arrived, staggering, to that country house upstate. Insect sounds swept over interstate. We walked

to its side, visible to the train tracks. That

wending gorge path goes past, now I know,

the house of someone I know. There

she was ready to greet us, in front. So well-known, unestranged still. Heat broke like a fever. The cold longness opened a threadbare space through which to push into the waxy speaking,

back & forth, rubbed into shine.

× × ×

Inside

the smell of balsamwood on the table's dark mahogany. We read poems out loud, became voicing in between. Heat

broke the shells. Heat broke the hinges—upper shoreface, lower, water becoming all a wave wall on the lake's grey, not sewn-in by colder needles to one block. And,

through it all

the middle ligament grew. It was growing the whole time. It grows in the background, in all backgrounds. It grows.

It chains us in a thread that contracts. We take our time. The couch

fits no one (heresy).

× × ×

The city expands. It takes in the cemeteries outside its walls. It carves into them freestanding stairwells garrisoned with clear, spring leaves. Me-leaves, you-leaves, Celan-leaves—him. They gather—all the spaces you measured gather there between the leaves.

What matters is what exists. First of all measuring the area of what exists.

I can make a word too. *Blätterspiel*, leavesplaying.

I can perceive the cucumber smell of the freshly broken banana stem.

Your language is *more sober, more factual . . . "grayer"* after—towing mine towards tolling.

After.

Friendship as a Way of Life

Every poem was a place where we could meet.

There was no difference between reading with you and writing with you. I said

I love how we write. Not in the obvious way, but the non-obvious way. It

wasn't a house.

It was a house that never ends. It was a house flooded with water. It was a room we never enter, dangling

from a string we don't understand. A room where we could sleep on the lace bookshelf and not touch each other in the mirror. Stained glass. Prepositions in the morning. Learn Old French beneath the bright, gothic walls, squeeze

juice out of oranges into the sink and eat only the peel.

A thousand-pointed star, even bitterness is new. Dazzling. Feminine.

Necessary to preserve.

Last winter I thought of this winter. We weren't friends yet. The postcards were in the drawer, exploding

forwards like wine in a glacier. Care has a direction. I know you'd love

to resurrect. As ballrooms. Frostbite. Finitude. I think that's ok. I think we would be fine without me. We would be relentless. I'd love

to just glue the floor to the ceiling one morning, in silence, a blank page. You could kill me. That's what invention means. This whole

time I couldn't see where you were. I tried to piece

together the broken plates into a corridor. They formed a dark blue star.

Articulation of Solace

We are mothering ourselves. We are articulating solace for each other. We are trying

to not fall in love. Write love poems

to not fall in love.

The fault line between the language of feeling and the language of catastrophe? We find it. Our common language. *Our white world.* We are trying

to write close to it. Even closer. Closeness

changes. Every poem was once impossible.

Medieval torture devices. Phalansteries. That's when it mattered. That's when you wrote it.

Your father's car speeds up the mountain like an unsent letter and you see someone dead

in your dream when he is still alive outside it. Aliveness

changes. The kind

of violence that can be taken back. The room

where someone not deadly realized they could care for you and didn't. Or did. Now you imagine it emptied. The kitchen

without a sink, windswept, glazed emerald-gold.

You could picture solace only by bright walls, you said. *By*, not *in*. A nearness.

We were dreaming about an apartment in the Mesozoic. A meadow on Neptune.

Thinking. This relationship. Between cold pomegranates and the porcelain bowl that didn't break as it held them. Solace. I

wanted islands instead of worlds. I wanted a new kind of ice. One to hold on to, lying in bed at noon. Bitter citrus grafting

like lightning onto my neck so I could be orchards as well. As well

as seeds

of thunderstorms.

What's the point of time if we're never out of it, knocking at your door, in landfall, in someone else's house.

I wanted *we*, in the second person. I wanted unimaginable solace, in the second person. I

wanted terrifying friends

to love me. You,

carrying away gorgeous bags of treasure every time we meet. Deadlight. Clearly we were not who we were. Clearly we were not dead. We were not

mistaken. I wanted to look exactly like you.

05.31.23

Later the table will be covered in pain. It will be buzzing with the one pain between the palette & the brushes, the rags & the birthday tulips—all leveled into pure space.

The familiar objects, in their mantles, notched—can you not imagine they are holding back for a later, even more complete, exposure? Will there not be something more than surface & volume & the genius of texture.

Generosity, in its capaciousness, is a better space.

Moten: *Gotta learn to see through things. Gotta learn to love being seen through.*

While you paint, when I write letters—to O, to P—I feel nothing separates us. I feel, by the force of my will, I am close to them as I need. This is maybe misleading. More & more I am in trouble with the letters, their current tendency to harden. The veil-white hardening like tunics of a chalky eye.

If there are no longer schisms, long fault lines, there will be nowhere to go. That at least must be sustained.

You are one next to me. This adjacency means something beyond intimacy, beyond pleasure. I'm uncertain—

we are all in the storm but you are in the thunder, in the air's night pattern of bone. And snow, out of season the snow tears through the page.

Most of all it feels good when you are awake. When you sleep I will think of you so you are awake.

for Gabby

Chryselephantine, Conviction

Infinite riches, wrote Marlowe, *in a little roome*. This is not a precise image because it forgets the interplay. It lacks the rigor of interplay. As if the great hidden treasure

could be enclosed in the room without altering the room. You need a more beautiful word for room. Rabid pride. You need to put someone in the room

with the treasure who hates treasure & loves the room—*infinite*

riches, wrote Lucie Brock-Broido, *in the smallest room*—she loves the richness. Hyperbole

has always made me think

of ethics, something about saying more than needed, more than meaningful. Perceptible. At

the limit everything gets connected into the limits

of a face. Which is just face. Touchable face. I

don't know the relationship

between the possible and the impossible but I know they have to come into contact. Commune. When

W was sick I recorded poems for her by Lucie Brock-Broido. From her first book, *A Hunger*. In Cambridge, for W

I recorded a poem in the dark and, when I listened to it, I realized I could hear how dark the poem was in the surround. Dripping with time.

⁙ ⁙ ⁙

Something arises.

From the moon, something that is a moon, but we didn't know about.

& our knowing nothing fits in the groove

& goes.

Extend the genre, lift the leg. Let the mouse run past. Let us go—sitting with you is good, let us go is better. What remains

is sensitive to what could happen.

Our form petrifies & flakes off. Space shines beneath, free at last.

Your life is more than me. It wakes in the night & walks. It is a giant, a researching angel, a feathered
die, *spin*. The seventh side opens—o, o, o, o, o, o, o.

I don't want to be something.

Something.

I promise I will not be something. but I will be.

On the dark carpet already I am.

x x x

Thank you, place.
The feeling has found its wick—& goes in.
I do not.
Do not, follow.

Special to come here, the edge of America
in winter,

before leaving.
The edge of the car breathes in fog. So do we. Car, fog. Close
each to where it does not
exist.
Or—it does not exist.
It was, the whole time, something else, was the texture
of the stone, pulled from the sea, dried bracken dressing it—

it became something else, something it was not.
But it was this.
This is better.

Come inside.
I do.

Spend time with me?
No.

We finish the box of cigarettes.

At night

the river confluences through my dreams & ends in the wall &
the entire wall

is filled with its bleating.

This room? This was part of the dreaming? It was the end of it, the end? It is over?

It oozes into my hair.
My clothes are packed. My true self flutters, hiding in the blinks. The head turns

& another face shows through from its cavern.

Your night in Seoul, I hope, is cavernous. Shades of bags wave behind lit glass bricks

like my chair at home, whistling in the window wind.

I have built the labyrinth.
I am coming to you, other.

Notes

- "Superject, Undercommons" was written in a period of reading Fred Moten & Stefano Harney (on the "undercommons"), Erin Manning (on the "superject," after Alfred North Whitehead), & Don Mee Choi (on the "antineocolonial").

- "Theory of Mesh" quotes my friend Yun Qin's letter, Rachel Kushner ("Duras with an *S*" & *The Flamethrowers*), & Mei-mei Berssenbrugge (note to the second edition of *Empathy*). The diagram is from Paul Klee's *Pedagogical Sketchbook*; it appears in Gilles Deleuze's *The Fold.*

- "Vézelay" was written while beginning to read Georges Bataille's *Guilty*; Bataille is buried at Vézelay.

- "Plenum" is after Denise Ferreira da Silva's use of G. W. Leibniz's term "plenum."

- "Poetics" quotes Clarice Lispector (*The Foreign Legion*) & Ingeborg Bachmann (*Malina*).

- "Flightpath" is after George Oppen ("Route") & ANOHNI and the Johnsons ("Cripple and the Starfish").

- "Tombpetals" was written for my friend R's exhibition "Tombstones" at Room 482 in Brooklyn. It quotes Roberto Bolaño (*2666*), Michel Serres (*Malfeasance*), Apichatpong Weerasethakul (*Uncle Boonmee Who Can Recall His Past Lives*), & Roland Barthes (*How to Live Together*); it also refers to Paul Celan's "Du liegst."

- "Listening" quotes Frank Bidart ("A Coin for Joe, with the Image of a Horse; c. 350–325 B.C.") & Stan Brakhage (*Metaphors on Vision*); it also refers to Jean Valentine's "The Windows."

- "Snakeskin" quotes Roland Barthes (*The Preparation of the Novel*).

- "Ithaca-Thiais" quotes Paul Celan ("Grösse, Glühende Wölbung") & draws from Pierre Joris's introduction to Celan's *Breathturn into Timestead*; Celan is buried in Thiais.

- "Articulation of Solace" was written while listening to Jenny Hval ("That Battle Is Over"), & reading Frantz Fanon (*Black Skin, White Masks*) & Paul B. Preciado (*An Apartment on Uranus*).

- "05.31.23" quotes Fred Moten (*from Day*).

Acknowledgments

With gratitude to their editors—versions of poems in this manuscript have appeared in the following publications:

- *The Baffler*: "Mouse Song"
- *Bennington Review*: "Flightpath," "Pasolini and Callas"
- *Denver Quarterly*: "Ithaca-Thiais," "Squall Path"
- *Duck*: ("Thank you, place . . .")
- *Georgia Review*: "Poetics"
- *Lana Turner*: "Friendship as a Way of Life"
- *Poetry*: "Theory of Mesh"
- *new_sinews*: "Consequential Maneuver," "Snakeskin"
- *Washington Square Review*: "Truant"
- *West Branch*: "Listening"
- *The White Review*: "Articulation of Solace"

× × ×

For my friends, some of whom are in these poems. I hope they are habitable places for you. In a true sense, I think there may be no rules. Thank you for everything.

For my poetry teachers—Jonathan Monroe, Patty Keller, Cecelia Lawless, Jorie Graham, Tracy K. Smith, & Josh Bell. Teachers, from the center of the labyrinth, pull your students in!

Thank you to the editors & everyone involved with this project at Nightboat. I am especially grateful to Santi for their help editing these poems with me.

Yongyu Chen is a poet;

their work has appeared in journals like

The Baffler, *Paris Review*, & *Poetry*.

They are working on a PhD in Film

& Visual Studies at Harvard

& live in London.